# WHAT BROUGHT THEM TO ISLAM?

THE CLEAR RELIGION SERIES - PART 8
EXCERPTED FROM (WHO DESERVES TO BE WORSHIPPED?)

NO DOUBT THIS LIFE IS AN EXAMINATION
WHICH NEEDS YOUR FULL CONSIDERATION
AS TO WHAT YOU WILL TAKE TO
YOUR FINAL DESTINATION?
ONLY TRUE BELIEF AND GOOD DEEDS ARE
YOUR WAY TO SALVATION
(Muhammad Sherif)

**MAJED S. AL-RASSI**

EDITED BY ANN RONAYNE
REVISED 2019

مركز أصول
Osoul Center
www.osoulcenter.com
THE CLEAR RELIGION SERIES

***King Fahd National Library Cataloging-in-Publication Data***

Al-Rassi, Majed Bin Suleiman
The Clear Religion Series part 8: What Brought them to Islam?. / Al-Rassi, Majed Bin Suleiman .- Riyadh , 2021

40p ; 12 x 16.5 cm

ISBN: 978-81-19946-24-2

1-Islam I- Tile
210 dc 1442/7846

**L.D. no. 1442/7846**
**ISBN: 978-81-19946-24-2**
**LI.**



مركز أصول
Osoul Center



+966 11 445 4900
+966 11 497 0126
P.O.Box 29465, Riyadh 11457
osoul@rabwah.sa
www.osoulcenter.com

# CONTENTS

# HONORIFIC PHRASES IN THIS BOOK

*(the Exalted): used after the mention of God/Allah to express: Glorified and Exalted is He*

*(bpuh): Blessings and peace be upon him; used after mention of the Prophet Muhammad*

*(pbuh): Peace be upon him; used after mention of any prophet or after mention of Angel Gabriel*

*(May Allah be pleased with her): used after mention of a female Companion of the Prophet*

## ABOUT THE WORD 'ALLAH'

Although the English word 'God' has often been used interchangeably in this book with the word Allah, there is a difference. 'Allah' is the word in Arabic that is translated as 'God'. However, 'Allah' has a much more precise meaning than 'God'. 'Allah' is not merely an Arabic term for the word 'god'. Instead, the root word of the word 'Allah' is *ilah*, which means 'a god'. There are countless numbers of made-up 'gods', but only One True God worthy of worship, Whose name is Allah. The word 'Allah' literally means 'the worshipped', or 'the God'. Allah is, thus, the proper name for the **only Being that is worthy of worship in truth**, the True Creator of the universe. By saying 'Allah', Muslims are, in essence, negating every other entity which people wrongfully worship, while affirming worship to Him alone. The name 'Allah' is how God Almighty has referred to Himself in the Quran, and how Prophet Muhammad (blessings and peace be upon him) also referred to Him. Therefore, in this work, the term 'Allah' will often be used in reference to this One and Only God Who is worthy of worship.

# INTRODUCTION

Every individual is born into a religious environment that is not necessarily in accordance with his or her choice; children are raised to follow the religion or ideology of their family, society, or culture. Even as new-born babies, they are assigned either the religion of their family or the ideology of the state; in some countries, the child's assigned religion is even recorded on the birth certificate. By the time individuals reach their teens, they have usually accepted the beliefs of their parents or their particular society. Since these beliefs have come to feel normal to them, they may give no thought to examining and possibly changing them.

However, individuals often encounter, or are exposed to, various beliefs and ideologies throughout the course of their lives, leading many to question long-held beliefs, traditions, or philosophical ideas. They begin to question the validity of their own beliefs. Seekers of truth often reach a point of confusion, especially upon realizing that the believers of every religion, sect, ideology, and philosophy claim to profess the one and only truth.

There are only three possibilities: 1) everyone is correct, 2) everyone is incorrect, or 3) only one is correct and the rest are incorrect. It is impossible for all of them to be upon the true religion because the fundamentals of all religions are different. On the other hand, to claim that they are all incorrect is to deny that Allah (the Exalted) revealed His will to humankind. This proposition will seem absurd to those who believe in a wise Creator. After all, why would Allah create human beings and not reveal a way to the truth? So **which religion is the right**

**one, and how can the seeker of truth come to know it?** This is the main subject of this work.

When beginning the search for the true religion, one should keep in mind the following four things:

Firstly, Allah has given us the ability and the intellect to discover the answer to this crucial question, which is also a life-changing decision: **What is the true religion?**

Secondly, Allah, the Most Compassionate, has not left us to go astray without any guidance. Indeed, He sent us prophets with scriptures to show us the right path.

Thirdly, we should always remember the underlying reason for this search: the everlasting life to come depends upon adopting the true religion in this life. This should be our ultimate motivation and a driving force to keep us searching until we are completely satisfied.[1]

Fourthly, we can only determine the true path and make a rational and correct decision if we willingly put aside all the emotions and prejudices which often blind us to reality.

Kind regards,

Majed S. Al-Rassi
Phone: 966 50 5906761
e-mail: majed.alrassi@gmail.com

1 The Bible, in its present form, confirms that seeking the truth is the main cause for salvation. In John 8:32, it has been stated, "and you will know the truth, and the truth will set you free." Muslims believe that the existing versions of the Bible contain elements of the original true message, although it has been altered significantly over time.

# WHAT IS MOTIVATING PEOPLE TO TURN TO ISLAM?

It is a fact that Islam is growing rapidly in the West and around the world. In the U.S. alone, the number of Muslims has risen dramatically, from about 10,000 in 1900 to at least several million people today. Here are four main reasons why non-Muslims become Muslims:

1. Islam teaches that all believers are equal in the eyes of God, and it forbids any form of racism or discrimination due to colour, land of origin, tribe, etc.

2. Islam does not have a religious hierarchy; there is no priesthood in Islam, so individuals have a direct relationship with God, without intermediaries. All Muslims are taught to do good and avoid evil and to educate themselves about their religion, and they go to reputable scholars for knowledge and advice.

3. Islam teaches that all its followers are considered normal human beings. No one is allowed to exalt himself or herself over others by claiming divinity, or to deceive the community by claiming to have a direct message and/or direct alliance with God, or to have spoken with God. No one can make the false allegation that God has taken him as a son and that as a result of that, people should follow this person blindly!

   Unfortunately, some members of the clergy utilize this concept to deceive their followers for their own personal benefit. An example is when they convince their followers that they cannot be questioned and are beyond reproach; some even solicit sexual relations from vulnerable individuals who come to ask them questions and/or seek forgiveness from sins through them.

I spoke to one young woman who turned to Islam after waking up from her sleep and discovering this huge lie and deceit… finally realizing that she had squandered her modesty and decency in the bed of a drunk clergyman!

4. Islam teaches its adherents to establish and strengthen their own direct relationship with Allah, where no intercession is needed from another person. In Islam, there is no church to act as an intermediary between an individual and Allah. It rejects the concept of seeking forgiveness of sins by confessing to a priest, an ordinary human being, who has no authority to absolve anyone of sin.

   Muslims must follow the guidance of God's law as it has been revealed, and this will lead them to success. If individuals err, they only have to turn to Allah, because He is the Oft-Forgiving, the Most Merciful. Islam frees the mind from barriers and roadblocks, granting its followers unobstructed access to Allah. It teaches that Allah is the only One from Whom people should seek forgiveness. He does not need intermediaries (in any form) standing in between, presenting themselves as the gatekeepers to Allah and contending that only through them may people have access to Him. Islam strictly rejects the man-made concept of confessing one's sin to a human being such as a "priest", and it rejects the act of seeking salvation through this person. Allah is All-Hearing, All-Seeing, Most Merciful, and Most Knowledgeable. He is All-Rich. He does not need intermediaries to convey people's needs to Him. People need only to raise their hands and say, "Allah, please forgive me; I promise to repent," and Allah will forgive them.[1] That's it!

In general, this direct relationship is a means of accessing Allah's mercy and forgiveness. This concept is logical and straightforward; anyone would naturally be pleased to hear and believe it.

However, Allah (God) warns humankind that He refuses to forgive those who associate partners with Him:

{Indeed, Allah does not forgive association with Him, but He forgives what is less than that for whom He wills. And he who associates others with Allah has certainly gone far astray.} *(Quran 4: 116)*

1 Islam teaches that one must repent for the sake of Allah only (not out of compulsion or to be seen doing so), stop committing the sin, sincerely regret it, and intend not to return to it.

# BEST DECISION SHE EVER MADE

Islam is often called the fastest growing religion, and each person who embraces Islam has a unique story and unique reasons. Despite widespread misconceptions about women in Islam, a growing number of women are finding that Islam is the true religion and the best way of life. Ann Ronayne's story is below; she welcomes emails from readers and can be reached at ann.ronayne1@gmail.com.

"Me? Go live in Kuwait? No way!" That was my reaction when my manager tried to persuade me to take a position in Kuwait. But I was to learn that {...the command of Allah is a decree of predestiny that is ever fulfilled.} *(Quran 33: 38)*[1]

I was born and raised in suburban Washington, D.C. in a Catholic family, and I attended Catholic schools. In the 1960s, the Catholic Church made major changes in its teachings in an attempt to be more modern; it tried to focus more on positive aspects and de-emphasize what was considered negative: punishment, regulations, abstinence from certain foods at certain times, etc. (Even so, Catholics in the West routinely ignored many of the rules that still existed, such as the prohibitions on contraceptives.) The Mass, which had always been said in Latin, was said in English instead. The nuns who taught us replaced their habits (modest dress) with modern clothes. Our religion classes had never involved reading the Bible, but now, instead of focusing on religious beliefs, they involved discussion of social issues and singing a lot of contemporary folk songs, as did the new Masses. It seemed strange that so much of what

1 This translation is taken from Hammad, *The Gracious Quran*.

we had been taught as the truth was now completely changed. Still, when we prepared for our first Holy Communion, we were taught that the bread that the priest was putting in our mouths was the actual body of Jesus (which would bleed if we were to bite it). For these and many other reasons, I doubted my religion and rejected it from a young age.

My decision was only confirmed as I learned more. If the trinity was such an important concept, why hadn't Jesus explained that clearly (and repeated it over and over again)? If God wanted to forgive us, He could have done that without coming to Earth Himself and being crucified to atone for our sins. Was it Jesus the man or Jesus the God who died on the cross, and how can God – Who has no beginning or end – die? If God did send His son (who was also God?) down to Earth to guide us, why would He neglect to give us the message during his thirty-three years, so that the truth had to be discovered and given to us later by Paul, who never even met Jesus?! If Christianity were the true religion, why didn't Jesus himself live and teach it?

For many years, I considered myself an atheist or an agnostic, but I was never concerned with choosing a label. I thought it was enough that I tried to be a good person, and I felt that nonbelievers actually did more good works because they didn't depend on any supernatural being for help. I never felt that I was searching for answers about the purpose of life or about religious beliefs.

After the Gulf War, I was working as a computer consultant when my company was offered a position in Kuwait which was perfect for me. My initial reaction was that I had no desire to go and work in a place where I thought women were treated as second-class citizens; after all, I had the usual stereotypes about women in a place like Kuwait. The manager on location assured me that the working environment was professional and that there were many bright women in the organization, including those who would be my supervisor and manager. I was eventually persuaded to take the contract for one year, thinking that it would be an adventure.

I soon learned that all of the stereotypes I had brought with me were wrong.

My colleagues were always friendly and respectful, and it occurred to me that it was almost the only environment I'd ever worked in where I saw no evidence of sexual harassment-not even any off-colour jokes or racy calendars hanging in cubicles. (It was certainly different from the atmosphere I'd experienced in the US military.) The women working with me were university graduates and were not shy about speaking out, and most chose to wear Islamic dress. Advertisements did not use women's bodies to sell products.

I was impressed to see the bonds among families and members of the society in general. When one colleague lost his pay check, all of the men quickly pitched in until they had collected the same amount of money for him. People also gave generously to the needy, both locally and globally.

When someone's mother called and said she needed something, the person would leave work to take her to the doctor or get what she needed. If a man's uncle died, all the men attended the funeral prayer; if a woman's aunt died, all the women went to visit her to give their condolences. When someone married or had a baby or recovered from an operation, an extensive network of family members, friends and colleagues shared that experience. Hospital rooms were large and even furnished with sofas and chairs to accommodate all the visitors.

The attitude towards the elderly was different from what I was used to, since extended families lived together, with several generations in one house; the children who didn't live in the same house came to visit often, if not daily. Grandparents had children and grandchildren living with them and were not left to live and die alone, or sent to nursing homes (which don't even exist). Older women were highly respected; they did not feel the need to make themselves look young and beautiful in order to gain self-esteem. Taking care of one's elderly parents was seen as a blessing and an opportunity for doing good deeds, rather than a burden, and care of one's parents is emphasized in the moral system of Islam. (This is not to say that non-Muslims in the West don't care about their parents, but there are different priorities and expectations. There is usually more of an emphasis on nuclear families and independence, with the elderly themselves not wishing to be a burden on their families.) In general, dealing with difficult situations was seen as a test and not a cause for despair. Taking one's own life was rare and also forbidden because only Allah has that right.

When the month of Ramadan came around, I was amazed by the idea that one billion Muslims around the world were fasting together-abstaining from food and drink every day from long before sunrise until the sun set. I joined them in fasting the entire month, although I had no intention of becoming Muslim and didn't experience the spiritual recharge that I would feel later as a Muslim.

At the time, I knew little about Islam, and I'm embarrassed to say now that I considered it a backwards religion which would only appeal to the ignorant masses. As I slowly realized that the stereotypes I had brought with me were all wrong, I became curious about the religion. As I learned more, I discovered that Islam was the reason for the moral system I had witnessed, and that these positive social aspects had been part of Islamic societies throughout the centuries. Even small things that had struck me-such as greetings given among strangers when one entered an elevator or an office-had their basis in Islamic teachings.

I got a Quran translation and some other books and began reading. Over and over again, I was surprised at what I found-and perhaps more by what I didn't find. I found a belief system which was rational and uncluttered, and I didn't find the oppression of women or terrorism that I had expected. I was attracted by the emphasis on social justice and standing up against oppression.

Obviously, the key question about religion is deciding whether or not it is true. Since this decision must rely on faith to some extent, how can we really know? One factor is the credibility of the sources; in the case of Islam, the most important source is the Quran.

I was struck by its scientific accuracy, demonstrated by statements which describe scientific phenomena that were not discovered until recently. I learned that the Islamic world had made major contributions to scientific knowledge and was the seat of civilization and learning while Europe was in the Dark Ages. Logically, I knew that an illiterate seventh century Arab could not have written this book himself. I began to question my idea that there was no Creator-that the intricate systems that made up the universe and its life forms could have developed randomly or that we were born, lived, and died with no purpose.

I was impressed that the Quran had never been changed over the years, so that the Quran we read today (in its original Arabic) is exactly the same as that revealed to Muhammad (bpuh) and passed on to his followers 1400 years ago. All Muslims memorize parts of it, and there are millions of people around the world who have memorized it in its entirety, so even if every copy disappeared today from the face of the earth, it would be easily recorded again. I couldn't help but to contrast that with the Bible, a collection of books written by various people over time; different Christian sects do not even agree on which books are included, and in some cases, scholars do not even know who wrote the books. We do not have the original sources, and there are different versions of the later sources. There are many contradictions, and the New Testament actually rejects many of the teachings of the Old Testament.

I was surprised to find out that Islam had the same roots as Judaism and Christianity, and that Muslims believed in the same prophets, including Abraham, Moses, and Jesus (peace be upon them all).

I began to understand why Muslims loved Prophet Muhammad (bpuh) so much, and I wondered why I never knew anything about him... never even knew that he was a historical figure about whom so much was known, and whose gravesite is known and visited. Authentic narrations from those who were closest to him describe him as a modest, truthful man who stood up for justice and against oppression.

I used to walk along the beach at night, looking up at the moon and stars and reflecting on Allah's creation, as the Quran recommended. I became convinced that the Quran must have been a message from God, but it took me a while to actually accept Islam… yet it was so rational and simple in its essence: one God, one Creator of the universe and everything in it, Who offered us guidance to make the best of our lives in this life and the next. Obviously, there are more details, but this sums up the Islamic beliefs, and one who accepts this is essentially a Muslim.

The concept seemed so pure and logical, especially when compared to the concept of the trinity, which cannot be explained rationally. There are three Gods, but they are one God? Jesus is both fully divine and fully human, so that he is all powerful yet experiences hunger and thirst and other physical needs? Moreover, this uncomplicated main principle of Islam – that there is one God – is repeated over and over again in the Quran, in the sayings of Prophet Muhammad (bpuh), and in the prayers of ordinary Muslims. If the trinity were the true essence of God, wouldn't it have been clearly explained and mentioned over and over again?

**In Islam, God is just; He does not hold any of us accountable for the sins of another, which we had nothing to do with.** There is no concept of original sin or of a crucifixion required to redeem all of us from that original sin perpetrated by someone else.

Of course, there were aspects that made me reluctant to make such a momentous change in my life. For example, although I understood the purpose and the benefits of Islamic dress, I couldn't imagine wearing it myself until I attended a Ramadan dinner at an organization for English-speaking Muslim women and met dozens of Western women who had converted to Islam, and who felt proud to dress this way.

For all the reasons mentioned above, and under no pressure from anyone, I came to the conclusion that the Quran was the word of God, and that Islam was the true religion.

On the day that I decided I was ready to officially declare my Islamic faith, I asked a co-worker to help me do so officially. There is actually no requirement to say this publicly or to get any kind of certificate; the declaration of faith is simply a matter of testifying that there is no deity worthy of worship except Allah and that Muhammad (bpuh) is his Messenger. It was a very moving experience, since I was essentially starting life over again, with a clean slate. It was undoubtedly the best decision I've ever made.

When we returned to the office, I went back to my desk and resumed work. It didn't occur to me that this was anything but a personal decision, and no one even knew that I was considering it... but my friend informed everyone, and to my surprise, I received congratulations from well-wishers for the rest of the day. That evening, she invited me to her aunt's house, and with only a few hours' notice, her mother, sisters, aunts, and cousins (most of whom I'd never met before) had a party for me, complete with gifts of Qurans, prayer dresses, gold, etc. Over the next days and weeks, I received dozens of gifts from co-workers (some of whom I had never met), friends, and acquaintances. I was very blessed, for I know that others who embrace Islam sometimes encounter many hardships.

In my feminist years, we spoke of 'sisterhood', but this was my introduction to true sisterhood. Muslim women considered me their sister, simply for the sake of Allah (God). Over the years, I've met so many amazing Muslim women of all nationalities and classes and educational backgrounds, and in our gatherings, we often talk about how blessed we are and how different our lives are from what many people think. It's hard to describe the feeling of standing in prayer, shoulder to shoulder with so many different women, knowing that we are sisters in Islam whether or not we even know each other.

It took me several weeks to build up the courage to wear the hijab (Islamic headscarf), but I found it liberating in a way that I hadn't expected. I was worried when I travelled to the U.S. wearing the hijab soon after becoming Muslim, but I needn't have been. Everywhere I went, I was greeted by other Muslims with the Islamic greeting *Assalamu alaykum* (Peace be upon you). I felt welcomed as a part of the worldwide Muslim community, and the hijab was what made that possible; if I wasn't wearing it, other Muslims would not have recognized that I was also Muslim and would not have offered those greetings.

I don't mean to claim that the Muslim community is some sort of utopia. Certainly, there are problems, but the problems are not from Islam; on the contrary, they are due to ignorance and rejection of Islamic beliefs and practices. The reality is that Islam does not need a reformation; Muslims do.

# OTHER MUSLIMS WHO WERE FORMERLY CHRISTIANS

There are many Christian women and men from all backgrounds who have embraced Islam. The following is just a small sample of well-known contemporary Muslims who sincerely studied Christianity before rejecting it in favour of Islam. They were chosen because their stories (as well as their books, articles, and videos) are easily accessible online in English.

**Dr Jerald Dirks** is an American former Methodist deacon (minister) with a Master's in Divinity from Harvard University and a PhD in Psychology from the University of Denver. The more he studied the Bible, the more he realized that he could not accept Christian teachings, and the more he dreaded going back to preaching what he knew was not true. When he took his questions to other ministers whom he respected, some of them admitted (behind closed doors) that they agreed with him, but they could not abandon their religion without breaking up their families and cutting off their livelihoods. Dr Dirks, along with his wife Debra, realized that Islam was the religion that actually followed the message brought by Jesus (pbuh) and other Prophets of God. Read more about them at http://www.jeralddirksanddebradirks.com/.

**Yusha (Joshua) Evans** was attending a Bible College in the southern United States, learning to read the Bible in Hebrew and Greek and intending to become a Christian missionary or minister. After reading the Bible cover-to-cover six or seven times, he was left wondering at the inaccuracies and inconsistencies he noticed. He left Christianity and began searching for the truth, but no religion satisfied him until he found Islam. See more about him at https://yushaevans.com/.

**Aminah Assilmi** (d. 2010, may Allah have mercy on her) was an American Baptist who found herself in a class with some Arab Muslims and decided to try to convert them to Christianity. When her attempts failed, she asked for a copy of their Quran so that she could read it and show them the error of their ways. After one and a half years of research, she ended up embracing Islam instead.

**Dr David Liepert** is a Canadian anaesthesiologist who started studying Islam with the intention of showing his Muslim colleagues that they were wrong and that Christianity was the truth. He sought to prove this by studying the Bible and trying to answer his own questions... yet he couldn't find the evidence to support his beliefs. His story is narrated in *Choosing Faith: Rediscovering the Commonalities Between Christianity & Islam*, which is available online at http://www.choosingfaith.com/.

**Idris Tawfiq** (d. 2016, may Allah have mercy on him) was a British writer and broadcaster who touched the hearts of many. He had a degree in English Language and Literature and taught in both the UK and Egypt. He also had a degree in Sacred Theology from the Pontifical University of Saint Thomas Aquinas in Rome; before embracing Islam, Idris was a Roman Catholic priest.

# HOW TO BECOME A MUSLIM

Every religion has its own requirements for conversion.

Someone who wants to become Jewish must pledge all of the following:

1. To enter the 'eternal covenant' between God and the people of Israel and to become a Jew of his or her own free will;
2. To accept Judaism to the exclusion of all other religious faiths and practices, which means to deny the prophethood of Jesus and Muhammad (bpuh) and to deny the revelations that God sent to humankind through them;
3. An undivided loyalty to Judaism and to the Jewish people under all circumstances;
4. To commit to learning the Torah and other Jewish knowledge; and
5. To raise his or her children as Jews.

To be a Christian, one must:

1. Believe that God (Allah) has a partner, a mother, and a son;
2. Believe that every new-born baby is born sinful;
3. Believe that God became a man and descended to Earth to die for the sins of the people;
4. Deny the prophethood of Muhammad (bpuh) publicly; and
5. Deny that the Quran is a revelation from Allah, the Exalted.

However, to become a Muslim is simple. One must:

1. Bear witness that there is no deity worthy of worship except Allah (in other words, disown all false gods),

2. Bear witness that Muhammad (bpuh) is His messenger,
3. Believe in all the six articles of faith, and
4. Worship Allah as taught by Prophet Muhammad (bpuh).

Hence, becoming a Muslim is a simple and easy process. If anyone has a real desire to be a Muslim and has full belief that Islam is the true religion of God, all he or she needs to do is to pronounce the *shahadah*, the testimony of faith.[1] Pronunciation of this testimony with a sincere heart brings the person into the fold of Islam. It is the main gateway to Islam.

Prophet Muhammad (bpuh) said:

«Whoever testifies that there is no deity worthy of worship except Allah, Who has no partner; that Muhammad is His slave and messenger; that Jesus is the slave of Allah, His prophet, and His word[2] which He bestowed in Mary and a spirit created from Him; that paradise (heaven) is true; and that the hellfire is true- Allah will eventually admit him into paradise, according to his deeds.» (Recorded by Bukhari)

The first part of the testimony consists of the most important words of truth that Allah has ever revealed to His noble prophets, "There is no deity worthy of worship except Allah." He has stated:

{And We sent not before you any messenger except that We revealed to him that: There is no deity except Me, so worship Me.} *(Quran 21: 25)*

---

1 The words of the *shahadah* are: *Ash-hadu al-la ilahailla Allah, wa ash-hadu anna Muhammadan Abduhu wa Rasooluhu.* (I testify that there is no deity worthy of worship except Allah, and I testify that Muhammad is His slave and messenger.)

2 It means that Jesus was created when Allah said the word "Be"; when He said it, Jesus was created in the womb of his mother, Mary.

Bearing this testimony implies that all forms of worship-whether praying, fasting, supplicating, seeking refuge, or offering an animal as sacrifice-must be directed to Allah and to Him alone. Directing any form of worship to other than Allah (whether to an angel, a prophet, Jesus, Muhammad [bpuh], a saint, an idol, a statue, the sun, the moon, a tree, a cross, or anything else) contradicts the fundamental message not only of Islam but of all the prophets; it is an unforgivable sin in the hereafter, so one must repent before death.

The second part of the testimony means that Prophet Muhammad (bpuh) is the slave and the chosen messenger of Allah.[1] This implies that a true Muslim obeys and follows the commands of the Prophet (bpuh) as mentioned in the collections of his hadiths. One must believe in what he has said, practice his teachings, and avoid what he has forbidden because the hadiths were, in fact, revelations and inspiration conveyed to him by Allah.

As mentioned earlier, Prophet Muhammad (bpuh) was sent in order to implement the Quran in a practical way through his sayings, deeds, and legislation, as well as all other facets of his life. When his wife Aishah (may Allah be pleased with her) was asked about his character, she replied:

«His character was that of the Quran.» (Recorded by Muslim and Abu Dawood)

Hence, to truly adhere to the second part of the shahadah is to follow his example in all walks of life. Allah has mentioned:

---

1 The meaning of worship is, simply, total submission and complete obedience to Allah's commandments in belief, intentions, statements and actions. This is what is meant by 'slavery to Allah' in Islam.

{Say [O Muhammad]: If you should love Allah, then follow me, [so] Allah will love you and forgive you your sins. And Allah is Forgiving and Merciful.} *(Quran 3: 31)*

A true Muslim must strive to mould his or her life and character to emulate the Prophet (bpuh), for he was a living example for human beings to follow. Allah has said to His Prophet (bpuh):

{And indeed, you are of a great moral character.} *(Quran 68: 4)*

Allah has also said to all people:

{There has certainly been for you in the Messenger of Allah an excellent pattern for anyone whose hope is in Allah and the Last Day and [who] remembers Allah often.} *(Quran 33: 21)*

When one enters the fold of Islam, all previous sins are forgiven; one starts a new life of piety and righteousness since he or she, in essence, has repented from the ways and beliefs of the previous life. One man told the Prophet (bpuh) that he would accept Islam only under the condition that Allah would forgive his sins; the Prophet (bpuh) asked him:

«Do you not know that accepting Islam destroys all sins that came before it?» (Recorded by Muslim)

As soon as a person accepts Islam, he or she is free of all previous sins. The person's record is wiped clean, as if he or she was born that very day. One should try as much as possible to keep his or her records clean and strive to do as many good deeds as possible; the more good deeds, the more he or she will be elevated in paradise.

It should be emphasized again that accepting Islam does not mean turning your back on the messages of previous prophets (peace be upon them all). Indeed, it is a fulfilment of those messages. Therefore, if you are a Jew or a Christian, accepting Islam and following Prophet Muhammad (bpuh) is a fulfilment of the messages which Moses and Jesus (peace be upon them) brought.[1]

On the other hand, rejecting Islam means turning your back not only on Prophet Muhammad (bpuh) but also on Prophets Moses and Jesus. Doing so is actually a clear violation of their messages, and it diminishes your hope of paradise in the hereafter.

It is now up to you to decide where your own future home will be. I wish you all the best!

1 This has been clearly described and proven in al-Rassi, *The Amazing Prophecies of Muhammad (bpuh) in the Bible: Twenty-Eight Proofs from the Bible of Muhammad's Prophethood.*

# CONCLUSION

**Islam is your birthright. Yes, you read correctly. Islam is your *right*.** Every human being is born into the religion of Islam, and human beings are naturally drawn to what we already know. Thus, if you accept Islam, you are not turning your back on any prior revelation but rather returning to the original pure belief with which you were created. This being the case, Islam is your birthright, whereas other religious or ideological systems teach you to deviate from the pure belief with which you were created.

# BIBLIOGRAPHY

Caraballo, Simon (Muhammad bin Abdullah Caraballo). *My Great Love for Jesus Led Me to Islam*. Jubail, KSA: Dawah & Guidance Centre.

Hammad, Ahmad Zaki. *The Gracious Quran.* Lisle, IL: Lucent Interpretations, LLC, 2008.

Liepert, David. Choosing Faith. Riyadh: International Islamic Publishing House, 2011. (Available online at http://www.choosingfaith.com/.)

al-Rassi, Majed. *The Amazing Prophecies of Muhammad (bpuh) in the Bible: Twenty-Eight Proofs from the Bible of Muhammad's Prophethood.* http://www.saaid.net/The-clear-religion/06.pdf.

Saheeh International. *The Quran: Arabic Text with Corresponding English Meanings.* Jeddah: Abul Qasim Publishing House, 1997.

*The Holy Quran: English Translation of the Meaning and Commentary*. King Fahd Holy Quran Printing Complex.

# APPENDIX

This book is excerpted from *Who Deserves to Be Worshipped?*, available at http://www.saaid.net/The-clear-religion/017.pdf.

**Also see the other excerpts:**

1. *What Is the Purpose of Creation?* http://www.saaid.net/The-clear-religion/028.pdf.
2. *The Beautiful Teachings of Islam.* http://www.saaid.net/The-clear-religion/029.pdf.
3. *Eleven Facts about Jesus and His Mother (Mary) in the Islamic Teachings.* http://www.saaid.net/The-clear-religion/04.pdf.
4. *Is Original Sin a Fact?* http://www.saaid.net/The-clear-religion/030.pdf.
5. *The Amazing Prophecies of Muhammad (bpuh) in the Bible: Twenty-Eight Proofs from the Bible of Muhammad's Prophethood.* http://www.saaid.net/The-clear-religion/06.pdf.
6. *Islam's Revival of Jesus' Teachings.* http://www.saaid.net/The-clear-religion/05.pdf.
7. *Is the Bible the Word of God?* http://www.saaid.net/The-clear-religion/031.pdf.

**For Further Information about Islam**

- Ata ur-Rahim, Muhammad and Ahmad Thomson. *Jesus: Prophet of Islam.* Riyadh: International Islamic Publishing House, 2008.

- Baagil, M. *Christian-Muslim Dialogue*. Riyadh: International Islamic Publishing House.
- Bucaille, Maurice. The Quran and Modern Science. Riyadh: International Islamic Publishing House, 2001.
- Ibrahim, I. A. A Brief Illustrated Guide to Understanding Islam. Houston, TX: Darussalam, 1997. (Available at www.islam-guide.com.)
- Khan, Maulana Wahiduddin. *God Arises*. Riyadh: International Islamic Publishing House, 2005.
- Khan, Abdul Waheed. *The Personality of Allah's Last Messenger*, 2nd ed. Riyadh: International Islamic Publishing House, 2007.
- LeBlanc, Abdul-Malik. *The Bible Led Me to Islam.* Toronto: Al-Attique Publisher.


**Online Information about Islam**

- islam-guide.com
- iera.org
- islamtomorrow.com
- discoveritsbeauty.com
- edialogue.org (live chat)
- islamhouse.com/en/ (thousands of free books)
- iera.org/shop/ (free downloads)
- iiph.com

# GLOSSARY OF ISLAMIC TERMS[1]

| | |
|---|---|
| *Abu* (or *abi*) | father (of) |
| hadith | a statement or action of Prophet Muhammad (bpuh) that was remembered and recorded by his Companions and followers |
| Hajj | the major pilgrimage to the Sacred Mosque, site of the Kaaba in Makkah, to be undertaken by every able Muslim once in his or her lifetime |
| hijab | veil ordained by Allah for believing women |
| Kaaba | the House of Allah in Makkah, originally built by Prophets Abraham and Ishmael |
| Ramadan | the ninth month in the Islamic calendar; the month of obligatory fasting |
| *shahadah* | the Islamic testimony of faith: *Ash-hadu al-la ilâha illa Allah, wa ash-hadu anna Muhammadan Abduhu wa Rasooluhu.* (I testify that there is no deity worthy of worship except Allah, and I testify that Muhammad is His slave and messenger.) |
| zakah | obligatory charity payable by Muslims, to be distributed to poor Muslims who qualify as recipients |

1 If a word has become part of the English language (i.e., is found in a dictionary of Standard English), that spelling is used in this book.

www.ingramcontent.com/pod-product-compliance
Lightning Source LLC
Chambersburg PA
CBHW062204160726
48282CB00027B/991
*9788119946242*